D0341576

Quotable Women

Quotable Women

A collection
of shared thoughts

Running Press
Philadelphia, Pennsylvania

A Running Press Miniature Edition™

Copyright © 1989 by Running Press.
Printed in Hong Kong.
All rights reserved under the Pan-American and
International Copyright Conventions.

Canadian representatives: General Publishing Co., Ltd.,
30 Lesmill Road, Don Mills, Ontario M3B 2T6.

International representatives: Worldwide Media Services,
Inc., 115 East Twenty-third Street, New York, NY 10010.

9   8   7

Digit on the right indicates the number of this printing.
Library of Congress Catalog Card Number 89-4299
ISBN 0-89471-756-1 (cloth)

This book may be ordered by mail from the publisher
Please add $1.00 for postage and handling.
But try your bookstore first!
Running Press Book Publishers
125 South Twenty-second Street
Philadelphia, Pennsylvania 19103

Imagination
is the highest kite
one can fly.

—LAUREN BACALL, b. 1924
American actress

Introduction

These quotations by women—that is, by politicians, performers, poets, mothers, daughters, temptresses, saints, and trailblazers—no more express a single viewpoint than would a similar collection of sayings by men. Some of these women voice the idealism that sustains them in their drive to succeed despite society's expectations; others comment on life with the wry pragmatism born of trying to juggle the roles of wife, mother, lover, friend, housekeeper, and worker. Some proudly convey a sense of self-worth; others find strength through their sense of humor.

Whether irreverent or inspirational, these observations share two qualities: a clear vision that reveals what is essential, and an affirmation of the joy of being alive.

$\mathcal{A}$ woman's life can really be
a succession of lives,
each revolving around
some emotionally compelling situation
or challenge,
and each marked off
by some intense experience.

—WALLIS, DUCHESS OF WINDSOR
(1896–1986)

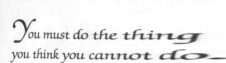

You must do the *thing*
you think you cannot *do*

—ELEANOR ROOSE~~VE~~
American stateswo~~man~~

$\mathcal{A}$nd the trouble is,
if you don't risk anything,
you risk even more.

—ERICA JONG, b. 1942
American writer

You will do foolish things,
but do them with enthusiasm.

—COLETTE (1873–1954)
French writer

*L*ife itself
is the proper binge.

—JULIA CHILD, b. 1912
American chef

Life begets life.
Energy creates energy.
It is by spending oneself
that one becomes rich.

—SARAH BERNHARDT (1844–1923)
French actress

One is not born a woman,
one becomes one.

—SIMONE DE BEAUVOIR (1908–1986)
French writer and philosopher

Life is what happens to you
when you're making
other plans.

—BETTY TALMADGE, b. 1924
American meat broker

I don't wait for moods.
*Y*ou accomplish nothing if you do that.
*Y*our mind must know
it has got to get down to earth.

—PEARL S. BUCK (1892–1973)
American writer

*A*voiding danger
is no safer in the long run
than outright exposure.
The fearful are caught
as often as the bold.

—HELEN KELLER (1880–1968)
American writer

*L*ook twice
before you leap.

—CHARLOTTE BRONTË (1816–1855)
English writer

$\mathcal{W}$hy not seize the pleasure at once?
How often is happiness destroyed
by preparation, foolish preparation!

—JANE AUSTEN (1775–1817)
English writer

$\mathcal{F}$ate
keeps on happening.

—ANITA LOOS (1893–1981)
American writer

Part of the trouble
is that I've never properly understood
that some disasters accumulate,
that they don't all land like a child
out of an apple tree.

—JANET BURROWAY, b. 1937
American writer

Trouble is a part of your life,
and if you don't share it,
you don't give the person who loves you
enough chance to love you enough.

—DINAH SHORE, b. 1917
American entertainer

*Courage is the price
that Life exacts
for granting peace.*

—AMELIA EARHART (1898–1937)
American aviator

Our strength
is often composed
of the weakness
we're damned
if we're going to show.

—MIGNON McLAUGHLIN
20th-century American writer

$\mathcal{Y}$ou can't be brave
if you've only had
wonderful things
happen to you.

—MARY TYLER MOORE, b. 1937
American actress

To live is so startling
it leaves little time
for anything else.

—EMILY DICKINSON (1830–1886)
American poet

. . . the greater part
of our happiness or misery
depends on our dispositions
and not on our circumstances.

—MARTHA WASHINGTON (1731–1802)
First Lady

I like living.
I have sometimes been
wildly, despairingly, acutely miserable,
racked with sorrow,
but through it all
I still know quite certainly
that just to be alive is a grand thing.

—AGATHA CHRISTIE (1890–1976)
British writer

*I*f you have made mistakes
. . . there is always another chance
for you . . . you may have a fresh start
any moment you choose,
for this thing we call "failure"
is not the falling down,
but the staying down.

—MARY PICKFORD (1893–1979)
American actress

Reality
is something
you rise above.

—LIZA MINNELLI, b. 1946
American actress

. . . *Some things* . . .
arrive on their own mysterious hour,
on their own terms and not yours,
to be seized or relinquished forever.

—GAIL GODWIN, b. 1937
American writer

$\mathcal{M}$istakes
are part of the dues one pays
for a full life.

—SOPHIA LOREN, b. 1934
Italian actress

Progress in civilization
has been accompanied
by progress in cookery.

—FANNIE FARMER (1857–1915)
American cook

$\mathcal{A}$ good cook
is like a sorceress
who dispenses happiness.

—ELSA SCHIAPARELLI (1907–1973)
Italian fashion designer

... that is the best—
to laugh with someone
because you both think
the same things are funny.

—GLORIA VANDERBILT, b. 192
American designer

$\mathcal{A}$ difference of taste in jokes
is a great strain
on the affections.

—GEORGE ELIOT (1819–1880)
English writer

The psychic scars
caused by
believing that you are ugly
leave a permanent mark
on your personality.

—JOAN RIVERS, b. 1939
American entertainer

Plain women
know more about men
than beautiful ones do.

—KATHARINE HEPBURN, b. 1909
American actress

One of the things about equality
is not just that you be treated
equally to a man,
but that you treat yourself equally
to the way you treat a man.

—MARLO THOMAS, b. 1943
American actress

$\mathcal{I}$t is hard to fight an enemy
who has outposts in your head.

—SALLY KEMPTON, b. 1943
American writer

She did observe,
with some dismay, that,
far from conquering all,
love lazily sidestepped
practical problems.

—JEAN STAFFORD (1915–1979)
American writer

We can only learn to love
by loving.

—IRIS MURDOCH, b. 1919
Irish writer

... him that I love,
I wish to be free—
even from me.

—ANNE MORROW LINDBERGH, b. 1906
American writer and aviator

*L*ove is not enough.
It must be the foundation,
the cornerstone—
but not the complete structure.
It is much too pliable,
too yielding.

—BETTE DAVIS
American actress

I don't need a man
to rectify my existence.
The most profound relationship
we'll ever have
is the one with ourselves.

—SHIRLEY MacLAINE, b. 1934
American actress and dancer

*J*ust remember,
we're all in this
alone.

—LILY TOMLIN, b. 1939
American actress

$\mathcal{I}$t is easy to be independent
when you've got money.
But to be independent
when you haven't got a thing—
that's the Lord's test.

—MAHALIA JACKSON (1911–1972)
American gospel singer

The most popular
labor-saving device
is still money.

—PHYLLIS GEORGE, b. 1949
American sportscaster

Always there remain
portions of our heart
into which
no one is able to enter,
invite them as we may.

—MARY DIXON THAYER, b. 1896
American writer

$\mathcal{T}$act is
after all
a kind of mindreading.

—SARAH ORNE JEWETT (1849–1909)
American writer

One of the oldest human needs
is having someone to wonder
where you are
when you don't come home at night.

—MARGARET MEAD (1901–1978)
American anthropologist

. . . Love from one being to another
can only be
that two solitudes come nearer,
recognize and protect
and comfort each other.

--HAN SUYIN
(MRS. ELIZABETH COMBER), b. 1917
Chinese writer and physician

I always felt
that the great high privilege,
relief and comfort
of friendship
was that one had to
explain nothing.

—KATHERINE MANSFIELD (1888–1923)
New Zealand-born writer

Fond as we are
of our loved ones,
there comes at times
during their absence
an unexplained peace.

—ANNE SHAW (1904–1982)
American writer

"*Stay*"
is a charming word
in a friend's vocabulary.

—LOUISA MAY ALCOTT (1832–1888)
American writer

*S*uperior people
never make long visits.

—MARIANNE MOORE (1887–1972)
American poet

. . . *Y*ou may be disappointed
if you fail,
but you are doomed
if you don't try.

—BEVERLY SILLS, b. 1929
American opera singer and manager

*Light tomorrow
with today!*

—ELIZABETH BARRETT BROWNING
English poet   (1806–1861)

*T*ears may be dried up,
but the heart—
never.

—MARGUERITE DE VALOIS (1553–1615)
French princess and scholar

$\mathcal{W}$e can do no great things—
only small things
with great love.

—MOTHER TERESA, b. 1910
Yugoslavian Roman Catholic missionary

In youth we learn;
in age we understand.

—MARIE EBNER—ESCHENBACH (1830–1916)
Austrian writer

$\mathcal{T}$ime—our youth—
it never really goes, does it?
It is all held in our minds.

—HELEN HOOVER SANTMYER (1895–1986)
American writer

The beauty of the world,
which is so soon to perish,
has two edges,
one of laughter,
one of anguish,
cutting the heart asunder.

—VIRGINIA WOOLF (1882–1941)
British writer

There's a time
when you have to explain
to your children
why they're born,
and it's a marvelous thing
if you know the reason
by then.

—HAZEL SCOTT, b. 1920
Trinidad-born American musician

Who knows
the thoughts
of a child?

—NORA PERRY (1831–1896)
American poet

Children require
guidance and sympathy
far more than instruction.

—ANNE SULLIVAN (1866–1936)
American educator

The only thing
that seems eternal and natural
in motherhood
is ambivalence.

—JANE LAZARRE, b. 194?
American writer

One never notices
what has been done;
one can only see
what remains
to be done.

—MARIE CURIE (1867–1934)
French scientist

Creative minds
have always been known to survive
any kind of bad training.

—ANNA FREUD (1895–1982)
Austrian psychoanalyst

To be successful,
the first thing to do
is fall in love
with your work.

—SISTER MARY LAURETTA
Roman Catholic nun

Think wrongly,
if you please,
but in all cases
think for yourself.

—DORIS LESSING, b. 1919
British writer

I am never afraid
of what *I* know.

—ANNA SEWELL (1820–1878)
English writer

It is the friends
you can call up
at 4 A.M.
that matter.

—MARLENE DIETRICH, b. 1901
German actress

J'll not listen to reason.
Reason always means
what someone else
has got to say.

—ELIZABETH CLEGHORN GASKELL
British writer   (1810–1865)

*W*omen are repeatedly accused
of taking things personally.
I cannot see any other honest way
of taking them.

—MARYA MANNES, b. 1904
American writer

*W*e don't see things
as they are,
we see them
as we are.

—ANAÏS NIN (1903–1977)
American writer

*A*ge is something
that doesn't matter,
unless you are a cheese.

—BILLIE BURKE (1886–1970)
American actress

$\mathcal{D}$on't compromise yourself.
$\mathcal{Y}$ou are all you've got.

—JANIS JOPLIN (1943–1970)
American singer

When choosing between two evils,
I always like to try the one
I've never tried before.

—MAE WEST (1892–1980)
American actress

A little of what you fancy
does you good.

—MARIE LLOYD (1870–1922)
English entertainer

One wonders
what would happen
in a society
in which there were no rules to break.
Doubtless everyone would quickly
die of boredom.

—SUSAN HOWATCH, b. 1940
British writer

$\mathcal{A}$ mother is neither cocky, nor proud,
because she knows the school principal
may call at any minute
to report that her child
has just driven a motorcycle
through the gymnasium.

—MARY KAY BLAKELY, b. 1957
American writer

Cleaning your house
while your kids are still growing
is like shoveling the walk
before it stops snowing.

—PHYLLIS DILLER, b. 1917
American entertainer

There are no more thorough prudes
than those who have
some little secret to hide.

—GEORGE SAND (1804–1876)
French writer

If it's very painful for you
to criticize your friends—
you're safe in doing it.
But if you take
the slightest pleasure in it—
that's the time
to hold your tongue.

—ALICE DUER MILLER (1874–1942)
American writer

In passing, also,
I would like to say
that the first time Adam had a chance
he laid the blame on woman.

—NANCY ASTOR (1879–1964)
British politician

Art is the only way
to run away
without leaving home.

—TWYLA THARP, b. 1941
American choreographer

The eye that directs a needle
in the delicate meshes of embroidery
will equally well bisect
a star with the spider web
of the micrometer.

—MARIA MITCHELL (1818–1889)
American astronomer and mathematician

I_f only
we'd stop trying to be happy,
we could have
a pretty good time.

—EDITH WHARTON (1862–1937)
American writer

Adventure is something you seek
for pleasure, or even for profit,
like a gold rush or invading a country;
. . . but experience
is what really happens to you
in the long run;
the truth that finally overtakes you.

—KATHERINE ANNE PORTER (1890–1980)
American writer

The only thing
that makes life possible
is permanent, intolerable uncertainty;
not knowing what comes next.

—URSULA K. LE GUIN, b. 1929
American writer

We all live in suspense,
from day to day,
from hour to hour;
in other words,
we are the hero
of our own story.

—MARY McCARTHY, b. 1912
American writer

I think that
wherever your journey takes you,
there are new gods waiting there,
with divine patience—
and laughter.

—SUSAN M. WATKINS, b. 194
American writer

RUNNING PRESS Miniature Editions™

Aesop's Fables
As A Man Thinketh
A Child's Garden of Verses
Emily Dickinson: Selected Poems
Friendship: A Bouquet of Quotes
The Literary Cat
Love: Quotations from the Heart
Quotable Women
Sherlock Holmes: Two Complete Adventures
Sonnets from the Portuguese
The Velveteen Rabbit

This book has been bound using handcraft methods, and Smythe-sewn to ensure durability.

The dust jacket was designed
by Toby Schmidt
and illustrated by Barbara Giles.
The interior was designed by
Judith Barbour Osborne.
The quotes were set in Zapf Chancery, and the
attributions were set in Triumvirate Thin by
Commcor Communications Corporation,
Philadelphia, Pennsylvania.